Gifts from Heaven

Based on true events

Written by
SUSANNE FUNK

Illustrated by
MARVIN PARACUELLES

Gifts from Heaven
Copyright © 2021 by Susanne Funk

All rights reserved. No part of this publication may be reproduced, distributed, or transmitted in any form or by any means, including photocopying, recording, or other electronic or mechanical methods, without the prior written permission of the author, except in the case of brief quotations embodied in critical reviews and certain other non-commercial uses permitted by copyright law.

tellwell

Tellwell Talent
www.tellwell.ca

ISBN
978-0-2288-5249-0 (Hardcover)
978-0-2288-5248-3 (Paperback)

Dedicated to my husband, children, and grandchildren:
You are my greatest gifts from heaven

From a very young age, Zoe loved to read. She loved adventure stories, but she especially liked true stories. Most mornings, Zoe had her nose deep in her Bible. Her favourite verse was Philippians 4:13:

"I can do all things through Christ who strengthens me."

Zoe loved God and was encouraged by how our All-Powerful God humbled himself to have relationships with the writers of the Scriptures. She knew that the Bible is the best way to discover how much God loves everyone, no matter what. Zoe was thankful that God still wants relationships today and that God was very interested in her life.

As a giraffe, she was unusually tall, and so she sometimes felt VERY awkward. She sometimes believed that she did not fit in with her friends. By accepting God's Son Jesus, who is Zoe's best friend, and by reading God's words, Zoe felt reassured that she was worthy of love and that she was beautiful and smart. She discovered that His Word was still the best way to meet Jesus, the Saviour of all. He loves her and everyone in this world: No matter how different or out of place one feels.

God is interested in your life and loves you, no matter what. How does this unconditional love that God has for you make you feel?

Zoe loved to study everything about God. She learned that in addition to the Bible, God loves using various ways to get one's attention. She discovered that God reveals himself through others showing love, helping and serving each other, through dreams and visions. God speaks to one's hearts in a still small voice, through nature; his imagination is limitless.

As well, Zoe read that God's Angels are used to serve as God's messengers to bless His creation.

On this warm summer day, Zoe read about a true-life story that angels sometimes drop pennies or dimes to reveal God's love and for us to experience hope in a problem situation.

"Pennies or dimes," thought Zoe. She smiled, whispering to herself,

"Oh dear Heavenly Father, You have an awesome imagination for sure."

How do you think God will bless you to get your attention?

After Zoe's first year of university and after spending much time in prayer, Zoe sensed God leading her to change her study direction and become a teacher. "I will need your help, God," she prayed often.

God kept His promise to bless her. To Zoe's delight, when she was 24 years old, she was hired to teach the most wonderful class of grade one students.

Now she was Mrs. Zoe.

Since she was different, it took some time for Mrs. Zoe to be accepted by everyone.

Nevertheless, she loved teaching, and her students and their parents adored her.

In the mornings, Mrs. Zoe especially loved to read a Bible story and have prayer time.

Starting the day with God set up the day just wonderfully.

As a matter of fact, story time was everyone's favourite part of the school day.

Mrs. Zoe read the most interesting stories. Most times, she made her students laugh or giggle, but sometimes she made them a bit teary-eyed during the sad parts.

Yet everyone knew that Mrs. Zoe picked the stories that were simply the BEST and always had a happy ending.

What is your favourite story?

While teaching, Mrs. Zoe especially loved helping those students who struggled in learning. She aimed to make sure that each student knew that they could accomplish very good things even if they felt different and left out.

Several years later, when Mrs. Zoe became a grade two teacher, she had a student named Dino in her class.

Dino had a very kind and soft heart, but she found learning math very hard.

"I don't get this," whispered Dino to herself.

Mrs. Zoe noticed Dino's pain.

What part of school do you find hard?

Mrs. Zoe spent extra time explaining the hard math to Dino. She showed Dino a new dinosaur math game board and little colourful T- Rex movers to help make the math clearer. Slowly, Dino raised her head. Dino straightened out her glasses and returned Mrs. Zoe's smile.

"I will try this," stammered Dino.

Mrs. Zoe smiled, stating: **"You are already a winner for trying, Dino!"**

Describe a time when someone has helped you be a winner.

In her class, Mrs. Zoe also had Connor, a black lab puppy, and J.P., a panda cub.

Connor loved to tease and laugh at J.P. who would often trip on one of his bamboo branches and **"Boom"** fall on his bottom. To make matters worse, Connor would then say: **"Watch out, Twinkle Toes!"**

Mrs. Zoe spent much time explaining the verse in Matthew 7:12:

"Do onto others as you would want them to do onto you!"

A little while later, J.P. finally had the courage to whisper into Connor's ear: "It hurts my heart when you laugh as I fall and when you call me names."

Connor was a good little puppy with a huge heart. He not only apologized but also promised to not do that again. "Will you forgive me, J.P.?" he asked quietly.

Thankfully, J.P. forgave easily. It always made his heart feel good to forgive.

How does your heart feel when you can truly forgive?

After further lessons on taking care of each other's hearts, Mrs. Zoe watched Connor explaining to Monkey how to be a good friend. She could see Connor holding Monkey's arm and placing it onto J.P.'s chest where his heart is. At the same time, Connor took J.P.'s arm and placed it on Monkey's chest.

"This is sweeter than an extra-large bubble-gum-sundae with a strawberry on top," thought Mrs. Zoe, smiling a big satisfied smile. "It is all about love! Oh, what joy it is to teach these student angels."

What else should a good friend do?

Several days later, however, Mrs. Zoe had a very miserable morning. She could not even finish her favourite breakfast. She had one of those days where everything very sad kept whirling around in her mind like a storm.

She kept thinking about how she was made fun of because of her unusual height and clumsy walking. Plus, her child made another poor choice and would not listen to her.

Mrs. Zoe felt that her prayers were not heard.

To make matters worse, she had hit her head on a tree!

Ouch!

Her heart and body hurt like having severe sunburn!

Needless to say, Mrs. Zoe came to school feeling like her love tank was completely drained.

Have you ever had a very sad day when you went to school? What happened?

Somehow, Mrs. Zoe managed to pull herself to the staff bathroom. She sat crying and crying on the toilet.

While sobbing, she thought: **"My life STINKS! I can't go to my class like this. My students deserve me to be happy and strong. They need me to love them. Oh, I feel so weak! Please, Jesus, HELP ME! HELP ME!"**

Mrs. Zoe prayed over and over again.

Has something ever made you so sad that you cried at school? Did you pray to God and asked for His help?

With her eyes swimming in tears, Mrs. Zoe realized in shock that the time on her watch said 8:45!

"I need to go to the classroom. The children are coming in soon," she whispered to herself.

<u>Be strong. Just go and sit at your desk</u>, a new voice from inside her told her heart.

"I can't," Mrs. Zoe thought.

But then, to her surprise, she found herself bravely opening the bathroom door.

Have you ever felt suddenly brave?
What made you feel brave?

Mrs. Zoe slowly slinked down the hallway and plunked herself on the chair by her desk. She was kind of numb from crying. With a bunch of toilet paper in hand, she blew her nose really hard.

Right after that, the first student entered the classroom. Connor bounced straight in and came to her desk with a big smile.

Jumping as if on a trampoline, he yelped, "Look, Mrs. Zoe: I found a penny and it's for you."

Connor handed Mrs. Zoe the penny. She felt special.

Mrs. Zoe smiled a weak smile and whispered, "Thank you. That is so kind of you, Connor! Your heart is as soft as a dove's down feather!"

Who could you make feel special today?

A minute later, in came J.P. He scampered straight to Mrs. Zoe and declared with a great, big grin, "Mrs. Zoe, I have a penny for you! Close your eyes and stretch out your hoof."

Carefully stepping forward so as not to trip, J.P. exclaimed: "Open your eyes!"

She smiled and locked eyes with J.P., and then they both stared at the penny.

"OH? Oh!" Mrs. Zoe declared, "THANK YOU! Two penny gifts within one minute. That is very cool."

Her heart was starting to feel a bit lighter.

What cool gifts have you received at school?

It was almost 9:00 a.m. Mrs. Zoe watched her students flock in. Almost everyone was present, except for Dino.

Thankfully, Dino finally arrived and she had the greatest and biggest smile on her face.

"I am so glad to see Dino so happy," thought Mrs. Zoe.

Dino, still holding her humongous smile, opened her backpack and took something into her hand. She held this "thing" in both hands behind her back.

Do you think it is another penny gift?

Slowly approaching Mrs. Zoe Dino whispered lovingly, "Mrs. Zoe, I found this at home and I thought you should have it."

Dino opened her hand and presented a beautiful angel to Mrs. Zoe!

Why do you think there is an angel gift now?

Staring wide-eyed at the angel, Mrs. Zoe exclaimed with a GREAT BIG SMILE:

"Thank you, Dino!"

At that very moment, a warm blanket-type feeling of **LOVE** came over Mrs. Zoe.

"This is so spectacular. I will always treasure your gift. You are my ANGEL!" She whispered to Dino, who blushed and felt extra special.

Mrs. Zoe sensed so much love all around her.

"God heard my HELP prayer! I am certain of it! I no longer feel this heavy sadness," thought Mrs. Zoe. "He strengthened me! My brain always knew that God loved me and that He would take care of me! This morning, however, my heart that was bursting with sad feelings took over my mind. I did not see things clearly and needed a direct reminder that God is very close and loves me."

Mrs. Zoe was now laughing to herself: "God must think I am a hard learner, or He knew my heart was very weak, so God sent THREE student angels to send me THREE gifts from heaven."

Will you try praying for God to send His help when you need it?

Mrs. Zoe turned the angel around and realized it had a pin.

'I wonder where I will pin this to always be reminded of God's unending and limitless love?'

Her mind was full of warm sunshine.

Seeing Mrs. Zoe so full of smiles made Dino, Connor, and J.P. want to be in a great, big group hug with their teacher.

Do you like group hugs?

How do you think Mrs. Zoe felt now?

Well, she felt amazing and her love tank now was so completely filled up that she could spread her teacher love to all these angels right in front of her. A deep peace settled into her heart, having renewed hope that her child would make better choices and others would start being kinder to her as well. She might even hit her head less often.

Mrs. Zoe stared at the angel and the pennies. These gifts from heaven gave her strength for the day while waiting patiently for His answers.

She recited her favourite verse to herself:

"I can do all things through Christ who strengthens me, Philippians 4 verse 13.

How do you think God will fill your love tank in the future?

With a warm smile, Mrs. Zoe gathered her class for story time and explained how God answers every prayer. Sometimes the answer is "yes," sometimes it is "no," and sometimes it is "wait". Since His creation has a tough time waiting for answers, God sometimes chooses to shower us with extra gifts that we need to feel strong again.

Understandably, the whole class, including Dino, Connor, and J.P.... and OF COURSE Mrs. Zoe... had a wonderful learning day!

Believe it or not: even math seemed to be easier, especially for Dino!

While teaching her class, beautiful thoughts kept rehearsing in Mrs. Zoe's mind:

"Thank you, Jesus, my best friend, for revealing yourself in the most interesting and fantastic way today! Yes, Jesus, I have renewed faith and can wait for your answers! You have the best imagination to reach us. I am so grateful for how You love finding unique ways to pour Your strength into us! You are the God of faith, hope and love."

1+1=
2+2=
3+3=

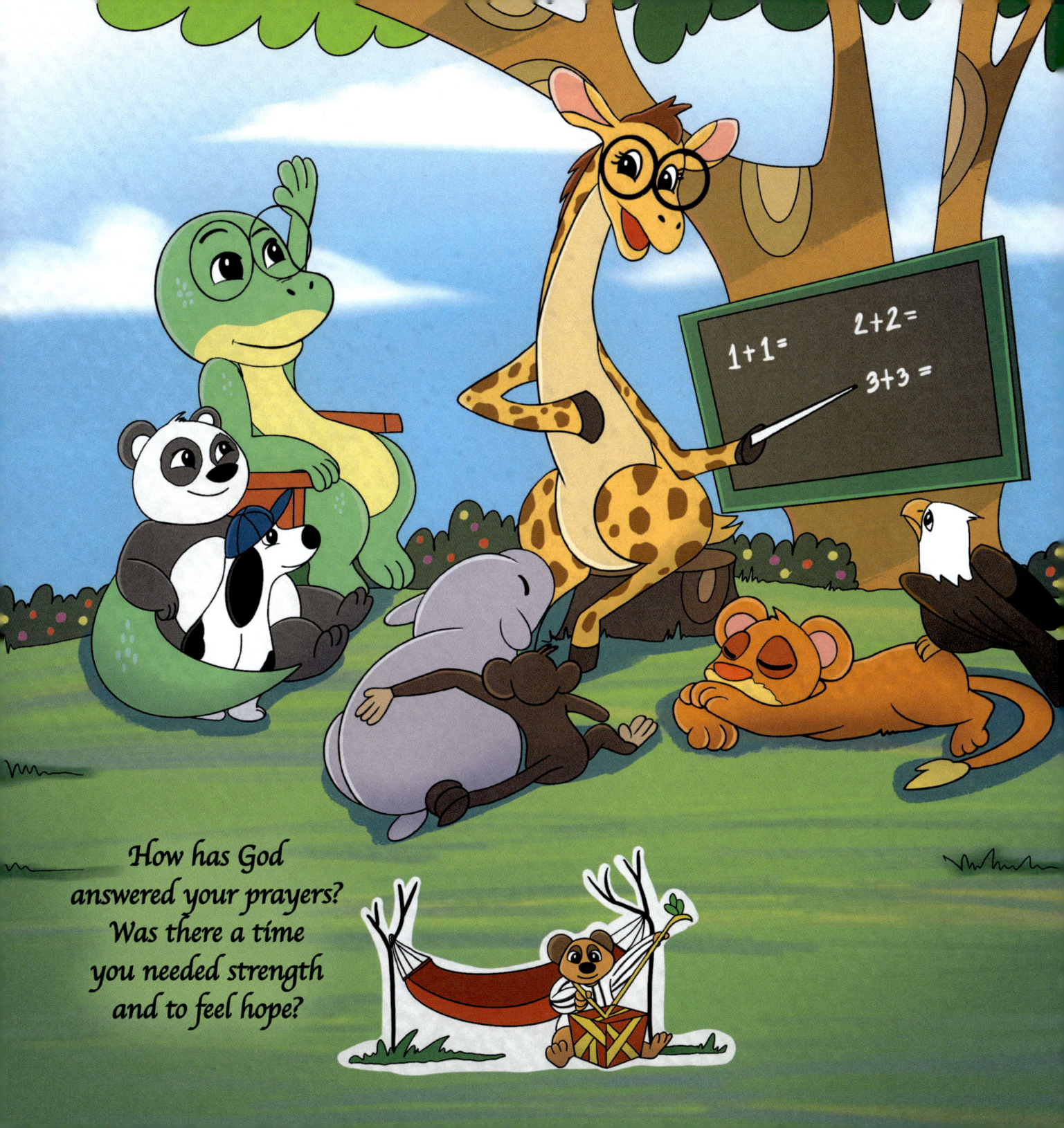

How has God answered your prayers? Was there a time you needed strength and to feel hope?

Things to Ponder

The written word of God, the Bible, is where one must always
look for God's love, hope, wisdom, comfort, and direction.
The gifts from heaven experienced by the author are extra
confirmations that God is not only real, but His actions are
also real. He can choose to answer prayers of HELP quickly!
Yes, God is very alive and active today!
You are encouraged to read the Bible and be
vigilant as you look for your signs.
You will know in your heart if an angel or angels have been
instructed by God to make you feel comforted and loved! God uses
three students in this true story to answer a teacher's prayer.
There is always hope!

Parents

This book lends itself to many readings. Each time one can recite Philippians 4:13, for example, and be blessed and strengthened by these words. Take time to recite different verses if you so wish. The questions on each page are often open-ended and can be used as springboards to important connection times with your child. It is okay if your child takes his/her time to open up about his/her emotions until further readings. You may also take time to share your own experiences to further bond with your child.
You do not have to use every question in the book.
The enjoyment of this book comes from its newness every time you open it. Also, it is the author's intent for the readers to discover that God is answering prayers and to share how He demonstrates those answers with one another. Once your child can read this story on his/her own, it will continue to be a treasure to be enjoyed for years.
In all of it, we want to give God the Glory.

Manufactured by Amazon.ca
Bolton, ON